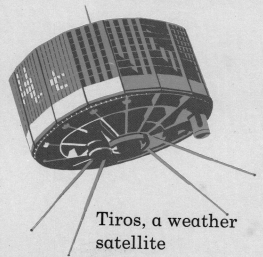

Tiros, a weather
satellite

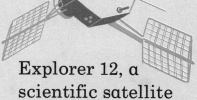

Explorer 12, a
scientific satellite

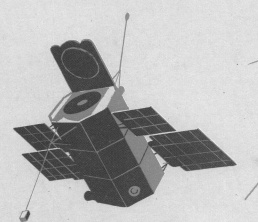

OAO, a scientific
satellite

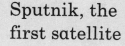

Sputnik, the
first satellite

First Published in 1970 by
Macdonald and Company
(Publishers) Limited
St. Giles House
49-50 Poland Street
London W1

Managing Editor
Michael W. Dempsey B.A.

Chief Editor
Angela Sheehan B.A.

Made and printed in Great Britain
by A. Wheaton & Company
Exeter Devon

MACDONALD FIRST LIBRARY

Into Space

Macdonald Educational
49-50 Poland Street
London W1

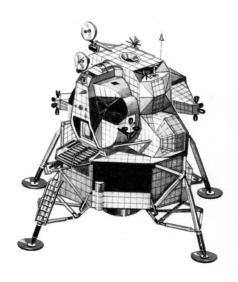

The clouds you see in the sky float in the
layer of air above the Earth.
This layer of air is called the atmosphere.
The Sun is far beyond the atmosphere.
It floats in space.
In space there is no weather.
There is no air.

At night you can see the stars and the Moon
in the sky.
The twinkling stars look very tiny.
But they are really big suns.
They look tiny because they are so far away.
The Moon looks much bigger than the stars
because it is much closer to the Earth.

Not long ago, nobody knew
what it was like in space.
Now men travel in
space, thousands of miles
beyond the Earth.
How do they get into
space and stay there?

If you throw a ball into
the air it will always
come down again.
The Earth pulls it back.
The harder and faster
you throw it, the higher
it goes.
If you could make the
ball go fast enough, it
would soar into space.

A rocket travelling at a speed of 18,000
miles an hour will go into space and stay
there.
At this speed it circles the Earth.
The path it follows is called an orbit.
To escape from the pull of the Earth, the
rocket must go even faster—25,000 miles an
hour.

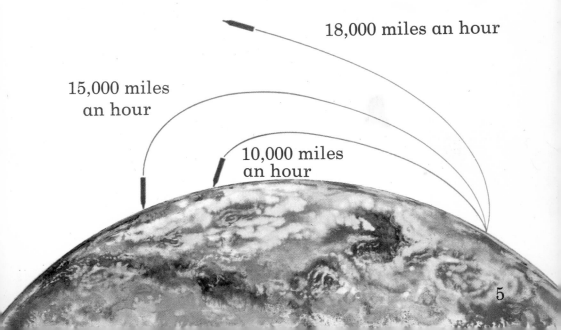

18,000 miles an hour

15,000 miles
an hour

10,000 miles
an hour

Firework rockets are the simplest kinds of rockets.
They burn gunpowder to make hot gases.

The hot gases shoot out of the end of the rocket and push the rocket forward.

The giant rockets which
soar into space work much
as firework rockets do.
But they are very much
bigger, as you can see.

This one takes men to
the Moon.
It is 364 feet high!

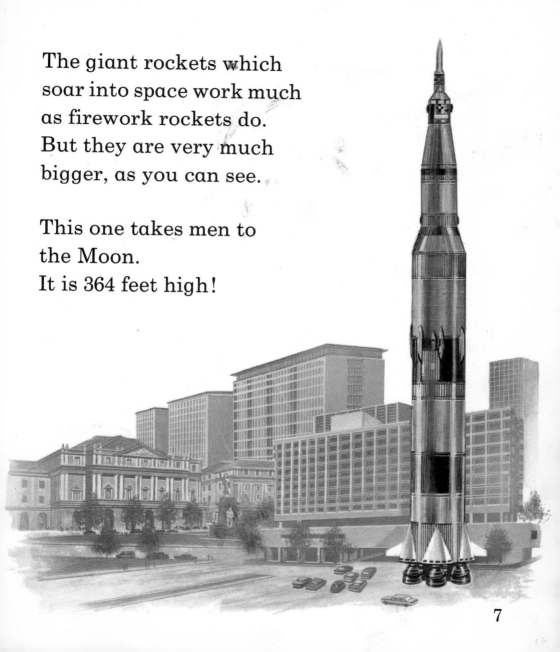

jet of
air

jet of
gases

Rockets burn their fuel
to make hot gases.
The gases rush through a
hole in the bottom of the
rocket and push it forward.
This is called jet
propulsion.

You can see how this
works for yourself.
Blow up a balloon and let
it go.
Just watch it fly!

The air rushes out of the
balloon and pushes it
forward.

One rocket is not powerful enough to lift itself into space.

A number of rockets must be joined together. Each one is called a stage.

The bottom stages give the top one a 'piggy back' into space.

They fall away when they have burned their fuel.

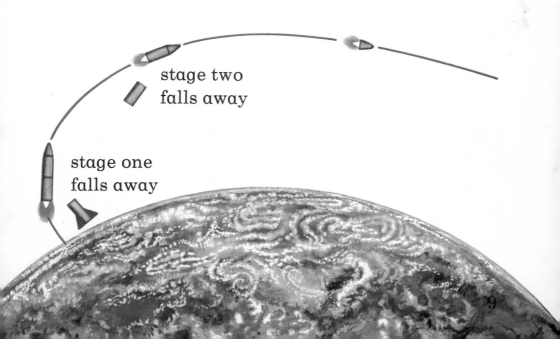

stage two
falls away

stage one
falls away

This picture shows the launching of a big space rocket.

Just look at the jet of flames coming from its powerful engines! The top part of the rocket will soon be travelling in orbit. We call an object travelling in orbit a satellite.

How does a satellite stay up in the sky?
It is like a stone being whirled round and
round on a piece of string.
The stone tries to fly away, but the
string pulls and makes it move in a circle.

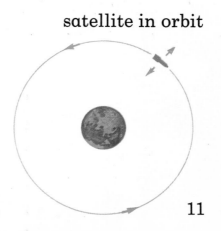

satellite in orbit

The pull of the Earth
makes a satellite move in
a circle, like the stone.
The pull of the Earth is
called gravity.

Satellites do many things when they are up
in orbit high above the Earth.
Some carry television cameras and take
pictures of clouds in the atmosphere.
They are called weather satellites.
The cloud pictures tell us what kind of
weather to expect in a few days.

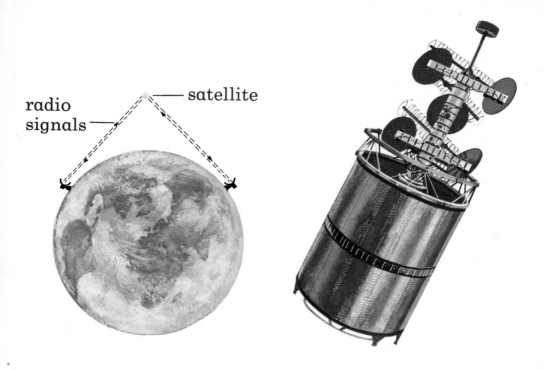

radio signals — satellite

Some satellites pass on radio messages and
television signals from country to country.
They are called communications satellites.

There is a communications satellite high
above the Atlantic Ocean.
It passes signals between England and America.

Men who travel in space are called astronauts.

The Russians call them cosmonauts.

The spacecraft astronauts travel in are much bigger than ordinary satellites.

They are made up of a number of sections.

The picture on the opposite page shows part of the Apollo spacecraft.

This carries three astronauts to the Moon.

The astronauts live in the top section.

It contains air for them to breathe.

Only this section comes back to the Earth.

The other section of the craft contains all kinds of equipment.

It contains batteries, rocket engines and fuel.

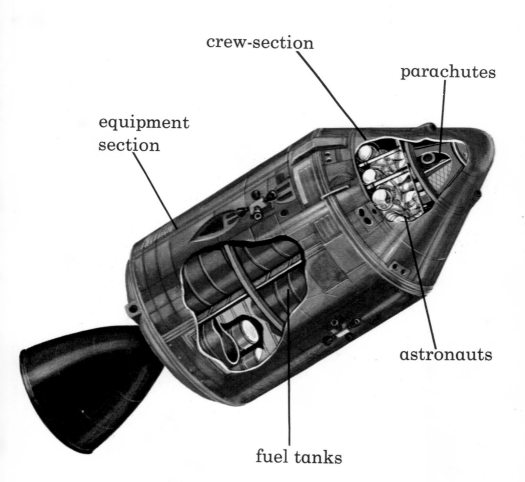

crew-section

parachutes

equipment
section

astronauts

fuel tanks

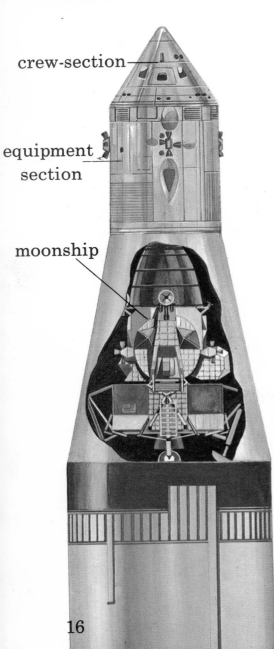

crew-section

equipment
section

moonship

The astronauts start
their journey into space
high in the air.
Their spacecraft sits
right on top of the
giant launching rocket.

The picture shows a
complete Apollo spacecraft
ready to go to the Moon.
The crew-section is at
the top.
The equipment section is
in the middle.
At the bottom there is a
separate little spacecraft
which will land on the
Moon.

The three astronauts enter the spacecraft.
They strap themselves to padded couches.
They must lie flat or else they would be
hurt by the strong push of the rocket.
Now it is time for blast-off.
The rocket fires with a great roar and lifts
the spacecraft up and up and up in the sky.

The spacecraft goes faster and faster as
each rocket stage fires beneath it.
After a while the final rocket is turned off.
Now the spacecraft is in orbit.
The astronauts have arrived in space.

When the astronauts unstrap themselves from
their couches, they find that they have no
weight!
They float about in the cabin.
Everything in orbit is weightless.

It is difficult to eat and drink.
Water will not pour from a glass.
The astronauts must suck it through a straw.
Their food is made into a paste.
They squeeze the paste into their mouths
from a tube like a toothpaste tube.

In space the astronauts usually breathe
the air in the spacecraft.
But sometimes they may have to go outside
the spacecraft.
They may need to check something or to make
repairs.

When they go outside they have to wear a
special suit.
The spacesuit gives the astronaut air to
breathe.
It protects his body and keeps him warm.

The suit is made up of a number of layers.
The top layer is made of very shiny material.
The helmet protects the astronaut's eyes
from the strong sunlight.

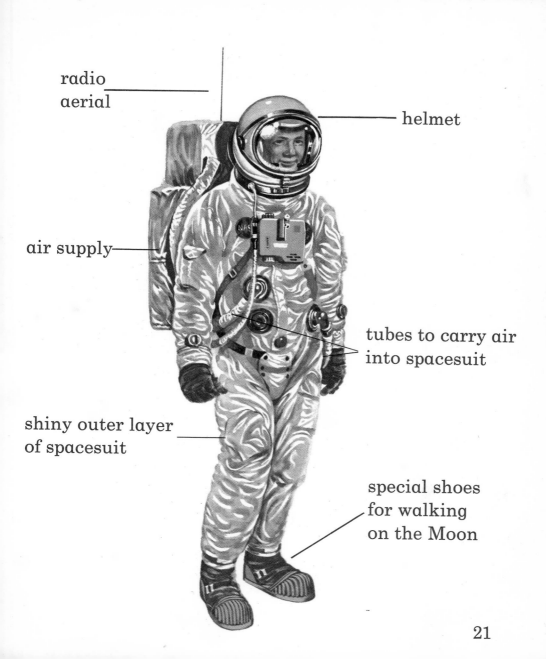

radio
aerial

helmet

air supply

tubes to carry air
into spacesuit

shiny outer layer
of spacesuit

special shoes
for walking
on the Moon

The astronauts stay in orbit for some time.
Then it is time to head for the Moon.
The astronauts fire the final rocket stage.
This makes the spacecraft go so fast that
the Earth's gravity no longer holds it back.
The astronauts turn their spacecraft so that
the moonship is next to the crew-section.

After about three days the astronauts are near the Moon.
They fire the spacecraft's engine backwards to slow them down.
Now they are in orbit round the Moon.
Two astronauts crawl into the moonship.
Then they fire the moonship's engine and it drops slowly to the Moon.
The crew-section stays in orbit.

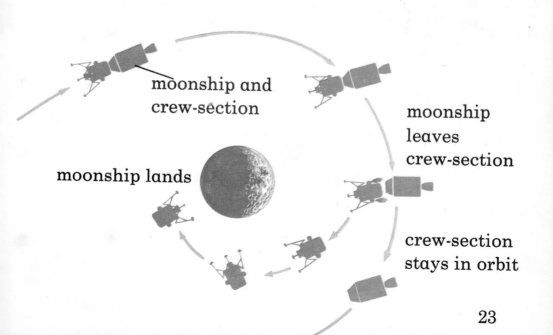

moonship and crew-section

moonship leaves crew-section

moonship lands

crew-section stays in orbit

The astronauts have landed on the Moon.
Soon they go outside to explore.
They must wear their spacesuits because
there is no air on the Moon.
Where there is no air, there is no life.
There is no sound.
The Moon is a dead, silent world.

All over the Moon there are lumps of rock
and great pits called craters.
The soil is soft and crumbly.
The astronauts leave big footprints.

They feel much lighter than they do on Earth
and cannot walk properly.

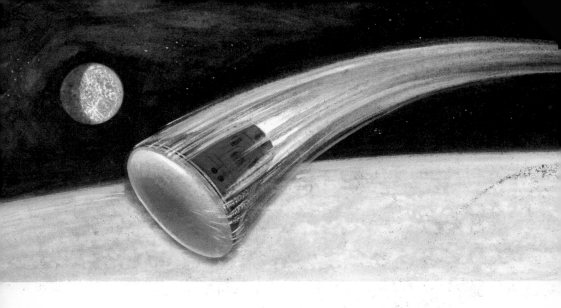

When it is time to leave, the astronauts
climb into the moonship and take off.
They join up with the other astronaut in
the crew-section and head for home.
The tiny crew-section of the spacecraft is
the only part to come back to the Earth.
It enters the atmosphere at great speed.
The air rubs against it and slows it down.
This rubbing makes the spacecraft red hot.

A few miles from the Earth parachutes open.
They slow the spacecraft down more and more,
and gently lower it into the sea.

Helicopters from a ship race to the spot
and pick up the astronauts.

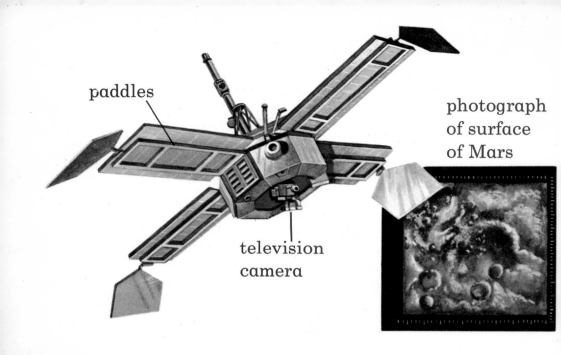

paddles

photograph
of surface
of Mars

television
camera

Some spacecraft travel far beyond the Moon.
They are called probes.
The probe in the picture went to the planet
Mars and took the photograph that you can
see next to it.
The probe has long paddles.
The paddles use sunlight to work the radio
and the cameras inside the probe.

Mars is a planet.

The Earth is also a planet.

There are nine planets, altogether.

Planets travel in circles round the Sun.

In the future, astronauts may travel to Mars and some of the other planets.

One day men may build space stations, which will stay in orbit high above the Earth.

They may look like this.

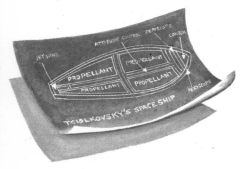

Konstantin Tsiolkovsky
was a Russian
school-teacher.
He was one of the first
men to think of using
liquid fuel in rockets.

Robert Hutchings Goddard
was an American.
He fired the first rocket
with liquid fuel.

Wernher von Braun was
born in Germany.
Now he lives in America.
He has designed many
American rockets.

Yuri Gagarin was the
first man to travel in
space.
He was a Russian pilot.

Alexei Leonov of Russia
was the first man to
'walk' in space.
He floated about outside
his spacecraft at the
end of a rope.

Neil Armstrong of
America was the first
man to set foot on the
Moon.
He stayed on the Moon
for over two hours

Index

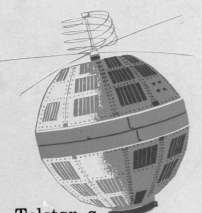

Telstar, a
communications
satellite

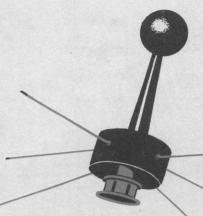

Explorer 10, a
scientific satellite

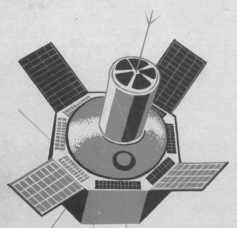

Cosmos, a
scientific satellite

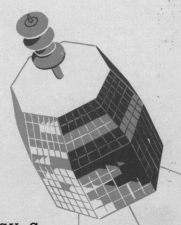

Relay, a
communications
satellite